Dedicated to my three amazing children, who have helped me see myself, taught me to love myself, and gave me hope that healing is ALWAYS possible.

Copyright © 2021 by Katie Brakefield

Because Sometimes Life Sucks.

An affirming journal/coloring/activity book for adults

This copy belongs to:

_____

Table of Contents

Introduction	1
Self-worth	7
Imagination Station	21
Attitude of Gratitude	35
Identifying Emotions	45
Unpacking Stress	63
Self-care	75

Introduction

Sometimes I want to work on myself and do all the things. Sometimes the idea of reading a self-help book or trying to journal like an actual adult is just exhausting. Sometimes I really want someone else to do the heavy-lifting for me so that I can hit the highlights and know that I did something positive for myself, even if it feels a little bit like I cheated. Welcome to my activity book where we are all a little weird and we are all a little broken, but none of us are nearly as alone as we think.

I read a lot- I mean like, a whole heck of a lot (okay, okay – two to five books a week); and mental health is my jam. I am a fan-girl of authors like Brené Brown, Glennon Doyle, Abby Wambach, Jenny Lawson, and many others. Throughout this book you will get snippets of wisdom from people I very much admire and who have changed my life in so many unbelievable ways. I hope you find comfort in their words (as well as mine), and take away something positive from the time you are investing in yourself. A recommended reading list is located at the back of the book in the event you would like to dive a little deeper into some high quality mental health books written by some amazing humans.

This activity book is what I wish I had available to me years ago, and since I couldn't buy one, I made one. This is a mental health book that you can skip around in and do what you feel like doing, or do a little bit from each section in order, or whatever floats your boat. There is a blurb for each section that gives you information about the subject and describes the following exercises for that subject. I recommend reading the blurb before jumping in so that you can get the most benefit possible. The "back" side of nearly every page in this activity book (or even numbered pages) is graph paper that can be used to sketch, journal, or doodle if the urge to do so comes upon you unexpectedly.

There really isn't a wrong way to use this activity book - be creative! Release the inner you - that young version of yourself that loves to color and make a mess and let their thoughts flow freely without worrying about what it looks like to someone else.

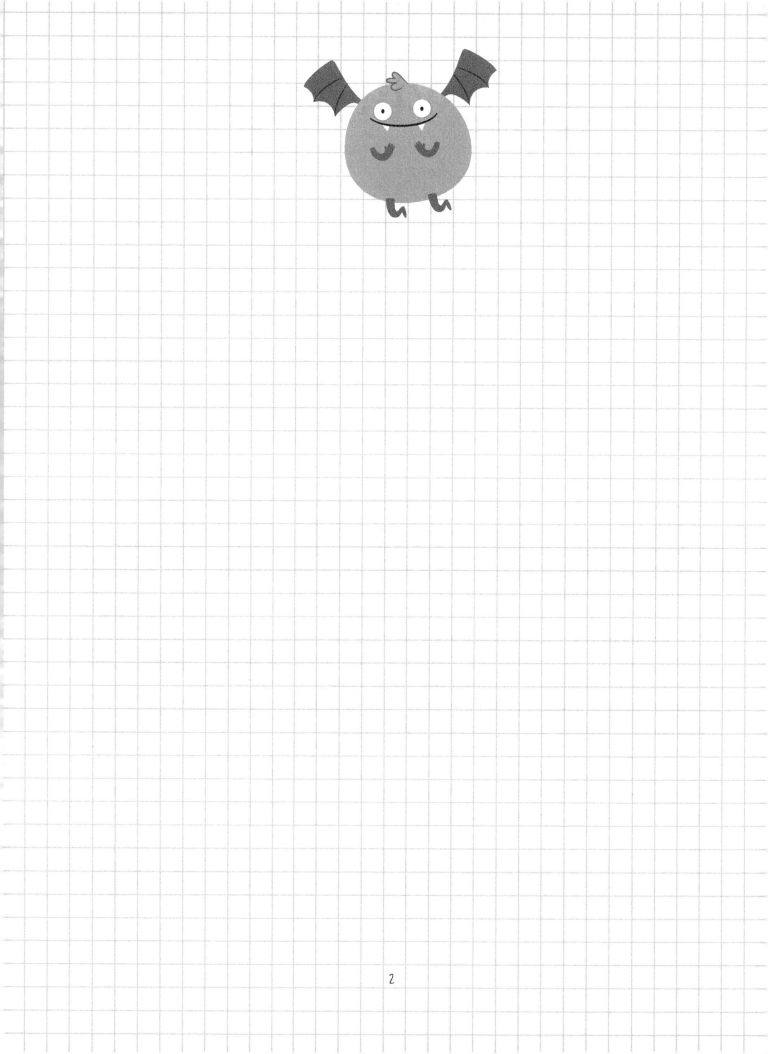

The activity pages in this book have a place for you to fill in the date. PLEASE write in the date so that when you look back at this book you can see your own amazing, miraculous growth (particularly during the really shitty times in your life). My therapist likes to remind me of how far I've managed to come, and that each step is worth noticing and celebrating! But we can't celebrate them if we don't recognize them. So much of our growth as adults is really difficult to identify because we are living it out every single day, and we often miss those subtle signs that we aren't quite who we were a week ago, three months ago, or a year ago.

Each mental health activity page will have four or five copies of each exercise so you can revisit the concepts on a somewhat regular schedule and see what changes for you. However, life gets nuts sometimes and you might set this down for a week that magically turns into six months - no judgement here. Take your time! The whole point is to do something positive for yourself and invest in becoming a better YOU. Some activities might be easier than others - **be gentle with yourself please.**

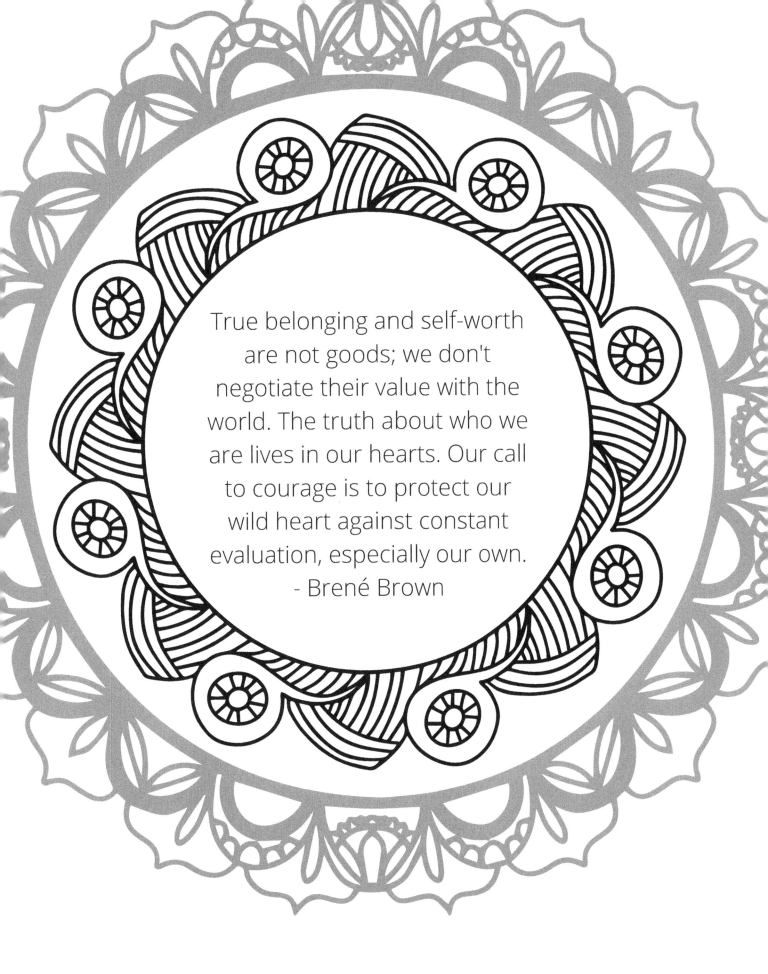

True belonging and self-worth are not goods; we don't negotiate their value with the world. The truth about who we are lives in our hearts. Our call to courage is to protect our wild heart against constant evaluation, especially our own.
- Brené Brown

Self-Worth

This is a sticky subject, and one that I feel lies at the very heart of most of our mental health issues: poor self-worth. We come by this deficit quite honestly: crappy (impossible to achieve) cultural standards, neglect and trauma in our growing-up years, abusive relationships, and lots and lots of shame. This lack of self-worth has super negative consequences in our lives and it shows up in lots of different ways. For example: how we allow people to treat us; our ability to create, maintain, and enforce healthy boundaries; the motivation and ability to complete self-care tasks (more on that later).

Think about self-worth like an electrolyte, let's say calcium. When we don't have enough, our whole body suffers. Calcium doesn't just effect the teeth or bones, but the heart, the brain, etc. And, just like Calcium, when want to increase our self-worth it is not just one dose and SHABAM, we're fixed. Nope. We gotta take some every day till we return to health, and then maintain those levels. It works the same way with our self-worth.

Think about how we assign value: does the "thing" belong in the trash, or does the "thing" deserve to be treasured? We wouldn't put a $10k ring in the trash just because it got a little dirty, but we would toss out an old t-shirt with a huge hole in it. Part of being human is assessing and assigning value to things and people. We assign value to art, relationships, items, places, etc. Some things have value because they remind us of better times (a.k.a. sentimental value), and some items have value because someone else told us they have value (the Mona Lisa). When it comes to self-worth, we get to decide if we determine our own value, or if we allow other people to assign our value. This is the difference between intrinsic (we decide our own value) and extrinsic (we let someone else decide our value) sources of self-worth.

Sometimes our intrinsic value is exceptionally low (due to things like: trauma, parental or relational abuse, substance abuse, etc.) so we seek validation of our worth from outside of ourselves, or we take the messages we've heard from others and internalized them into our intrinsic value. This can manifest as people-pleasing behavior or co-dependency and can lead to hustling for our worth EVERY DAY. It totally sucks for multiple reasons: it often means that we will accept whatever price-tag other people put on us (even if it is low because their "low" is still higher than our highest value of ourselves); that much hustle is exhausting and takes up all our energy. Working that hard to convince others of our value is a never-ending, full-time job and often requires us to play twister with our soul. So let's change the narrative!

SelfWorth

```
R N X B T U I K M R Z A U S E O C V H P K L J T M
A W W L O J L P G C Y N Z D S V T U E U L P B P C
V G Z L Y X J Z N N J Y G R B C Q T A E L S D L Y
E Z O W T K O Y I X H G U O N E I M C R Z E G C B
J D R S A J D J L N V C O Y I S R X G O J V W N
L C E S X O G C A E E B H O L B Q E O M K U X E W
H Y K Y V R R D E D V A W G Z A B K H Q W H S I F
Y E I I I F F S H V H O Q M T L O G W K R S S A F
B I V L P C N W E H R G L M U X J E A J L E B P E
R S S Y T P J F W T L L E F A T I M X E C E E P Y
A D G I L W Z I H R A Q E K E R D U K T A B U R D
V T Z K A P C Y B N T C R G D P Q D H U P G D Y R
E C D V C M X Q P Z A F F K P Y F S T Z A T S L O
K V F J G I R M T E A C Y M D Z H I M W B F O X C
D B G Y I P H Q P V H V B G F Z F T M Z L O B A H
L R H U E U Q I N U I E L E M U R V Z T E F N A W
C S H A E Y K U F N H V N R L F Z X N Y F I P Y C
G Z Q R C E Q G K P J V O Z O Q Z E H I F P W X Q
W W L M G K F R G F F T D V F D D K S J Y B R P R
B U Z W T D X F U I G W G P Q I T S W F K C P J S
W N U Y T B R X O T M N I Q F J S Y E X J U F N N
Q R Q D W Y P P I C P W I N B Z D G D E R Q M V U
Z F G D C C R E Z B X K O V U O R P O K P X H P X
V H J A E H W F S J J C J S O U H X E X N F N F W
K Y Z Z Z Q A I C E H K R H G L T F Q O B U B V B
```

BEAUTIFUL
BRAVE
CAPABLE
COFFEE
TEA
CONFIDENT
ENOUGH
FREE
FUZZY
HAPPY
HEALING
LOVELY
LOVING
PEACEFUL
UNIQUE
WEIRD
WISE
WORTHY

 It's totally okay if you don't know how you feel about all this. Go as slow as you need to, and know that baby-steps are highly undervalued in this world.

Date: _____

SELF-WORTH SHAKE-UP

1 -- 100

I AM TRASH   DAMN, I AM AMAZING

Place a mark where you are now, and a star where you would like to be.

Messages about my self-worth:

I am: (Ex. No one can truly love me because I am so broken, I just scew up everything I touch).
_____
_____
_____

WHEN I HEAR THIS MESSAGE IN MY HEAD IT SOUNDS A LOT LIKE _____.
(a parent/partner/boss/sibling?)

Would I feel comfortable saying this to my best friend/child/pet?
YES   or   NO

This message makes me feel:
(ex. It feels like I will never be good enough or heal enough to be fully seen or understood)
_____
_____
_____

If I could change this message, even a bit, to something that feels more positive, it would be:
(ex. I have been through so much that has been damaging to me and I am doing my best to heal every single day)
_____
_____
_____

Phew, that was hard work. Good job! Take a little break and color a flower:

YOU CAN'T JUMP FROM SELF-HATE TO SELF-LOVE,
SO LET'S START WITH A LITTLE SELF-ACCEPTANCE
AND SEE WHERE IT TAKES US.

PS: IF YOU ARE TELLING YOURSELF SOMETHING YOU WOULDN'T TELL YOUR BEST FRIEND/CHILD/PET, THEN YOU SHOULDN'T BE TELLING IT TO YOURSELF.

Date: _____

SELF-WORTH SHAKE-UP

1 -- 100

I AM TRASH   DAMN, I AM AMAZING

Place a mark where you are now, and a star where you would like to be.

Messages about my self-worth:

I AM: _____

WHEN I HEAR THIS MESSAGE IN MY HEAD IT SOUNDS A LOT LIKE _____.
(a parent/partner/boss/sibling?)

Would I feel comfortable saying this to my best friend/child/pet?
YES   or   NO

This message makes me feel:
_____
_____
_____
_____

If I could change this message, even a bit, to something that feels more positive, it would be:
_____
_____
_____

Yep - you guessed it! Time to color some more!!

13

Date: _____

SELF-WORTH SHAKE-UP

1 -- 100

I AM TRASH   DAMN, I AM AMAZING

Make a mark where you are now, and a star where you would like to be.

Messages about my self-worth:

I AM: _____
_____
_____
_____

This message makes me feel:
_____
_____
_____

WHEN I HEAR THIS MESSAGE IN MY HEAD IT SOUNDS A LOT LIKE _____
(a parent/partner/boss/sibling?)

Would I feel comfortable saying this to my best friend/child/pet?
YES   or   NO

If I could change this message, even a bit, to something that feels more positive, it would be:
_____
_____
_____

You weren't going to complain about more coloring, were you?

Why is it so easy to be hard on ourselves, but so hard to go easy on ourselves?

SELF-WORTH SHAKE-UP

Date: _____

1 -- 100
I AM TRASH   DAMN, I AM AMAZING

Place a mark where you are now, and a star where you would like to be.

Messages about my self-worth:

I AM: _____
_____
_____
_____

WHEN I HEAR THIS MESSAGE IN MY HEAD IT SOUNDS A LOT LIKE _____.
(a parent/partner/boss/sibling?)

Would I feel comfortable saying this to my best friend/child/pet?
YES   or   NO

This message makes me feel:
_____
_____
_____
_____

If I could change this message, even a bit, to something that feels more positive, it would be:
_____
_____
_____
_____

Hey - at least I'm consistent...color some more!

This is really hard work, and I'm proud of you.

HARD WORK IS IMPORTANT.
SO ARE PLAY AND NON-PRODUCTIVITY.
MY WORTH IS NOT TIED TO MY PRODUCTIVITY BUT TO MY EXISTENCE.
I AM WORTHY OF REST.
- GLENNON DOYLE

The Power of Imagination

I know I'm not alone in this...I've lived inside my own head for most of my life (or inside of a book). My imagination is agile, strong and more than capable of convincing me of things that aren't necessarily true. As human beings we are hard-wired to tell ourselves stories about what is happening to us (check out Brené Brown's Netflix special). We try to make sense out of how we are being treated, especially as little kids. When we are growing up and our primary care-givers are not present, are neglectful, actively abusive, or under the influence of substances that alter their personality, we are biologically programmed to try to justify why "bad" things are happening to us...AND we try to protect ourselves by imagining what might come next so we can be more prepared the next time the "big bad" happens, and maybe we avoid some of the hurt. This is a wonderful coping mechanism for surviving childhood trauma; its not so great for thriving as an adult.

This type of growing-up trains our brains to focus on all the different ways that things can go wrong. It was helpful back then; not so much when we want to change things up. Our mission, if we choose to accept it, is to teach our brains a new way to imagine. I won't lie to you, it is extremely uncomfortable in the beginning. Parts of me believed that by changing what I was imagining, I was jinxing myself, or cursing myself. Heck, I think most of us spend our lives waiting for the other shoe to drop when things go well. We ANTICIPATE disaster, plan for it, and imagine all the ways that life could turn into a dumpster fire. Guess what? We can change that!!!

The following section contains some of my favorite tools for transitioning out of the Negative Imagination Station and into something that is far more satisfying. We are often told we need to "stop daydreaming", but today we are going to start making it a daily practice. Spend a few moments everyday imagining something fun, beautiful, or exciting for yourself; then start working through these pages. Our imagination is one of our most POWERFUL tools. We can take something from our mind and make it real. It is our super-power. Let's not let it go to waste, or use it's power for the dark side.

Gentle Reminder:
We are looking at some very vulnerable parts of ourselves.
You might notice fear, discomfort, pain, anger, and/or other emotions.
Be present with those feelings. Acknowledge them.
And ALWAYS be kind to yourself.
Your emotional response to these exercises is VALID.

"Imagination is the beginning of creation.
You imagine what you desire, you will what you imagine, and at last,
you create what you will."
- George Bernard Shaw

It's okay to rest when you get tired.

Date: _____

Let's start with some basics...

It can be hard to find a positive jumping off point for our imaginations, so we will start with some things that we are actually good at already - .they can be big things or little things, but acknowledge some of your strengths.

Shit I'm Good At

Shit I enjoy doing:
Knowing what we actually enjoy doing is also a helpful place to begin.

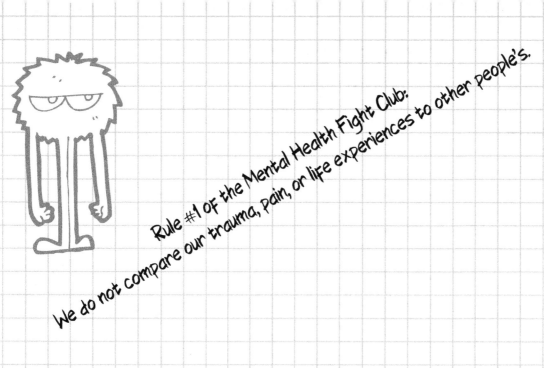

Rule #1 of the Mental Health Fight Club: We do not compare our trauma, pain, or life experiences to other people's.

Imagination Station

I want you to imagine the best outcome that you can about the following subjects (as if there were no financial, time, or other constraints), and then look inside of yourself for what limiting beliefs might be holding you back from achieving that dream. It can be tricky figuring out what the objective truth is about your limiting belief, particularly if you have trouble believing in yourself and what you can accomplish. The key with "next steps" is to NOT overthink it. I'll go first so you can see what this exercise looks like.

My dream job: I am a published author who tours the US and speaks about parenting teens with trauma, recovery from abuse, and the healing journey.

Limiting belief: No one will want to read my books because I don't hold any degrees or other qualifications in mental health, and no one will be interested in what I have to say about those topics.

Objective truth: My experience is valid and I am not the only one who has been through this or will go through this. Validating my own experience will validate other's experience. I am not a fraud, even if my feelings tell me I am.

Next steps: Continue working on the Adult Activity books; follow-through with publishing; write 1 hour/day.

Date: _____

My dream job: _____
_____

Limiting belief: _____
_____
_____

Objective truth: _____
_____
_____

The next steps: _____
_____
_____

Date: _____

My ideal relationship: _____
_____

Limiting belief: _____
_____
_____

Objective truth: _____
_____
_____

The next steps: _____
_____
_____

You are a gift to the world. There is no one who can give the world what you can.

Imagination Station

Date: _____

Thing I want to change: _____
_____

Limiting belief: _____
_____
_____

Objective truth: _____
_____
_____

The next steps: _____
_____
_____

Date: _____

Thing I want to change: _____
_____

Limiting belief: _____
_____
_____

Objective truth: _____
_____
_____

The next steps: _____
_____
_____

Date: _____

Thing I want to change: _____
_____

Limiting belief: _____
_____
_____

Objective truth: _____
_____
_____

The next steps: _____
_____
_____

My Perfect Day

Date: _____

If I could create a "perfect" day it would look like this:
(sketch it, describe it, make a collage, or whatever works for you)

Yes! Another word search

IMAGINATION

```
K S G E Z E S T Q S Q V H L Q X P Q W A C C R D Y
Y X Y J H H U Q G X Q T E R Y Y Q U Q D F Z E S N
P B V O G F P C U E K Z Q F P D R E A M S U D Z
K H D A S U E D G R X S N O M Y P W Q G Q Z C C T
K M Y L X K R T T N E T N O C O J I N H S Q A Z M
D P N G K J P R V H S R P E N E M N J O F R C V H
S T B U Z U O E A B F Y I F W P F P U O V N E B J
D Y X Y G A W F W Y G Y D E D A W Y I F T E P E J
I Q T K H P E W U Q T X J L N C E C P M R G L H P
Y J X F C S R M E F B O I M Q S T O K A O A W P C
Q Q K M Z K W A Z K Y W Y G J L S Z E N X T T O L
P U M X P V A C N D R D F R M I X R F I H I Z R T
D M B T O K F A O F K K Z Z T Q Q T K F T V L T P
T U R M G G P E E N D X B I W J D X C E X E E S C
F P N L M G I M G U N R V Y Q L V V I S S G H A N
O F M H G K W A J E A E L Q O Z U V L T A C S A A
U D E O Z T W X M V N C B K Q F Q U A K Z C A A
V X C A R R E O E I G X J T S G N Y L T G Z H C M
F Q A G R Q B R V I R T L D I S Y N B I D C L T O
C W H M O Y Y E H M Z K D H C O E T Y O E F S Y U
V W K G C I W K E R R Z B M L A N N X N S Y B T K
E X F G A S D E K O D N I R T G D S L R I D A I F
N F S O E Q A U V R Z X E X V B I D L R D Z C Q
U V S S E N D L O B T W N R B D I D Q H E J L G L
S O D F D U L H H N K V W F E S M V X L N W G P D
```

DREAMS
CATASTROPHE
CONNECTIONS
BRAVERY
BOLDNESS
POSITIVE
NEGATIVE
SUPERPOWER
MANIFESTATION
FEAR
JOY
WELLNESS
DESIRE
CONTENT

Breathing Break!
Drop your shoulders
Unclench your jaw
Deep breath in......
Pause...
Blow it out...

Why Gratitude?

If you've spent any time recently working on your mental health, you might notice that developing a practice of gratitude is pretty much everywhere you look. There are multiple reasons that developing this habit in your life is worth doing. In the previous section I talk about the power of our imagination - gratitude is one of the ways that we can transform our PHENOMENAL COSMIC POWERS (bonus points if you know what movie that's from) of imagination into something that serves us better than our old survival tactics.

The human brain is trained to look for patterns, and those of us who have been through trauma are already pro-level at predicting doom in our lives. We wanna change this, right? I want you to think about what happens when you get a new car, let's say it is a silver passenger vehicle...all of a sudden you see silver cars everywhere! It is the same with our thought processes and our imagination. We are already well trained to see all the "bad" stuff in our lives; all the things that hold us back, or make our lives difficult. It is time to change the narrative, to start noticing new patterns! Gratitude is the path we can take to do this.

The kicker is that we are NOT going to let this lead us to toxic positivity. We are not going to pretend that everything is sunshine and roses in our lives; instead we will gently sift our daily life for those experiences, people, or things that lifted us even a little, that brought a little light to a shadowed corner of our soul, or that made us feel better in the present moment. This is going to feel uncomfortable and maybe a little fake when you start. That's normal when you are developing a new skill. Stick with it! Don't give up! It is perfectly acceptable to start small. These do not need to be massive statements about how you *love* your whole life and everything is great - we know that just isn't the truth; but we can also be grateful for the first stretch of the morning where your spine elongates and your breath comes just a little easier, or the hot shower that released some tension in-between your shoulder blades, or the flower growing through the cracks in the sidewalk that made you grin because you kinda feel the same. It can be the hug from your teenage son who just isn't very touchy, or a compliment from a stranger about your new shoes. Pause and feel that feeling; stretch it out for just a minute. Worth it.

Gratitude tells us that we are in the present moment; The Now. We are not stuck, hopeless and abandoned in our old traumas or old ways of doing life.

Gratitude

```
E E R V U P P R G F Y M D T E Y Z R A L O R Z O W
M R H N A C H O S F D S O X J B X R L T Y D M R J
Z X C F X K B W V N V U C D K U F A T C T W Q N C
W I Y W O S H D G M N N E C G B R I K N I K Q Z E
C D T R F C L S J G R S A L Q R A N B Q C U H A T
Q S J L A N P P G F U H N U N J A B L J U A Q A A
C Q A K T L Q W M W M I Q F J A Y C D T H A F U L
Y W F U A Y I C Y S G N Y K L A T V I G J L D R O
B E A E S F W P D Q X E P N J O A U G O Z S X W C
K O Z M N P I E B E R G Y A N C Q S R V U R W O O
C S X M I V D K F T A S G H A L T U T E A S H A H
K A H P A W P X O U L W D T F P N R P V M U O F C
H C U T T N C U F J D X I N H S E Z J Z D J X V M
K Q D Q N A C A Q D N O B A E E Z C U W J T X O Q
D H O A U H B U L X N B W I T I R C Z P M F G T J
E W B J O T I E D I T W T T Q B R A K F N R V K W
E O N C M E V W K Z P T E E C A Q F P P C M E U C
B E L S T A I G B H M P S I X B U D A I L U X H E
U R D N R Y F Z O W G L W T G R P W L W S C Z M J
S S P T V H X E O K R G L N C U R J M Z O T L I Z
O R C C Y J J W K P E O Y W R F M A H J Z E K F P
P E A C E E M P S S A C F V R B R E A T H I N G H
Z T I A R F E H C P O W Y M U E A H E H O J S N F
K I D D O S W E J W R P Q H W L L R I D J S D V K
U U X K N A T O D K E Y E U D N W Z Q A W L G K N
```

THANKFUL
GRACIOUS
FRIENDS
NATURE
CHOCOLATE
NACHOS
BOOKS
MOUNTAINS
OCEAN
VACATION
THERAPIST
KIDDOS
FURBABIES
PEACE
QUIET
BREATHING
SUNSHINE
RAIN
TRAVEL
TOUCH

37

It sucks that discomfort is a necessary part of growth - but I am SO proud of you for jumping in anyway.

Attitude of Gratitude
Write down one thing you're grateful for each day!

Date: _____

Date: _____

Date: _____

Date: _____

Date: _____

Date: _____

Date: _____

Sometimes we just feel grumpy, and that is 100% okay...we can still be grateful too.

Attitude of Gratitude
One a day!

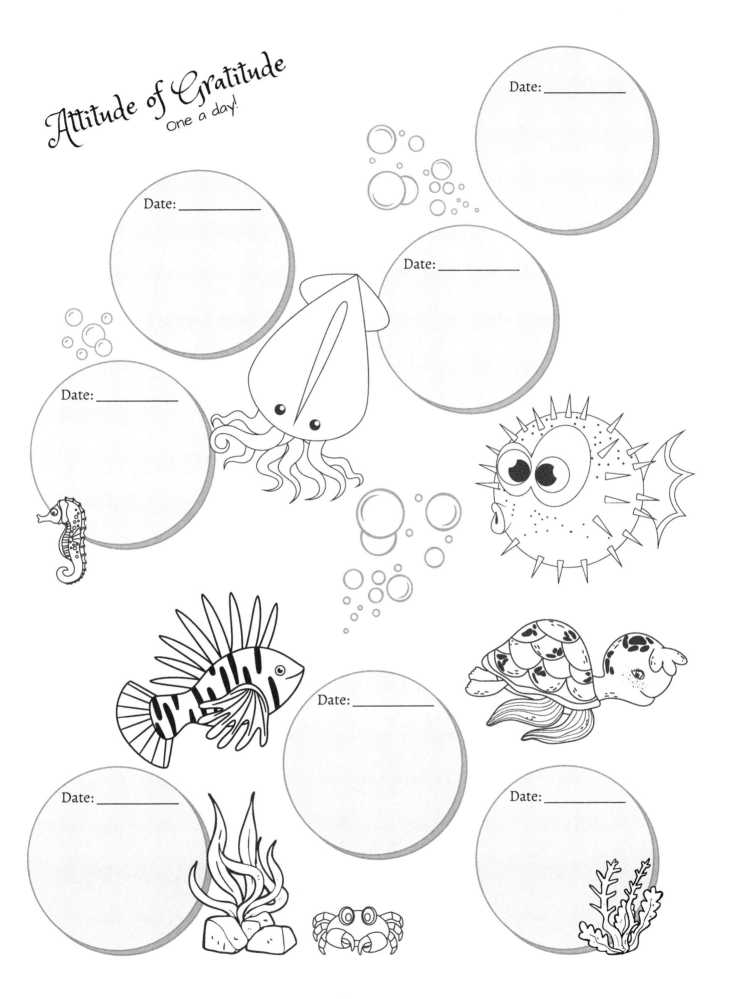

Stop feeling guilty about your "guilty pleasures" - You get to enjoy what you enjoy.

Attitude of Gratitude
One a day!

Date: _____

Date: _____

Date: _____

Date: _____

Date: _____

Date: _____

Trusting
   yourself
      can be
         scary;
            Take the next step anyway. You are worth it.

 # Identifying Emotions

I will happily admit that when it comes to emotions I am firmly in the Spock camp of emotional regulation - you know, ignore them until they go away, or stuff them way the hell down where they can never be found again. Turns out this is maybe not the healthiest way to manage your emotions. If you grew up like I did, then it wasn't safe to have or express certain emotions. We didn't have the luxury or time to explore them and thus understand them.

Addiction, co-dependency, abuse - these all take away our freedom to feel our emotions in a safe way, or learn how to self-regulate (learning how to calm ourselves and move from high states of emotion back to our baseline) so we find ways to deal with them in unhealthy ways. When we spend our whole lives smooshing emotions this way and that way, we can have some trouble identifying them once we become adults. They start coming out sideways and cause harm to the people in our lives that we don't really want to damage (spouse, children, friends, family). The problem is that even if we chose not to "feel" our emotions they are still there, sitting in our bodies, trying real hard to make themselves known. Sometimes this can manifest as illness, chronic fatigue, migraines, or autoimmune issues. Sometimes it just makes us assholes and we have a hard time forming healthy relationships.

Because I spent most of my formative years cramming those unsafe, messy feelings into a deep dark corner of my soul, I had extreme difficulty finding them again. Since I couldn't just yell "here fishy, fishy!" to my emotions and understand them, I found it immensely helpful to figure out where different emotions like to hang out in my body. One example: stress likes to camp out between my shoulder blades and make those muscles pretend like they're rocks. After I figured out where I was experiencing emotions in my body, it took me a little longer to be able to name what the emotion was. I started with the body outline found in many of my nursing text books. I used colors, textures, and/or labels and then kept adding to my understanding of my own emotional state. This has allowed me to be present for my own emotions, process them more comfortably, and act in alignment with myself. Emotions are just information. There is no moral value one way or another in regard to emotions - they aren't good or bad. They just are.

Here are some examples from my own practice with this exercise. See what you can come up with for your "feeling map". Remember there are no wrong answers - simply listen to and honor what your body is telling you.

1.) Shame for me feels like I just drank something too hot too quickly - like a red feeling that goes from my mouth to my stomach. It also makes my stomach feel like it's rapidly falling to the floor.
2.) Fear feels like grey concrete that locks my feet into place, and makes the hairs on my neck try to crawl off my head. It can also feels like I have something stuck in my throat, and my hands turn icy.
3.) Happiness feels like bubbles in my head, or like wrapping a towel straight from the dryer around my body.
4.) Stress feels like the sound that my old dial-up modem used to make when I would try to get on the internet. It is a heavy feeling on both sides of my shoulders and a tightness around my forehead.

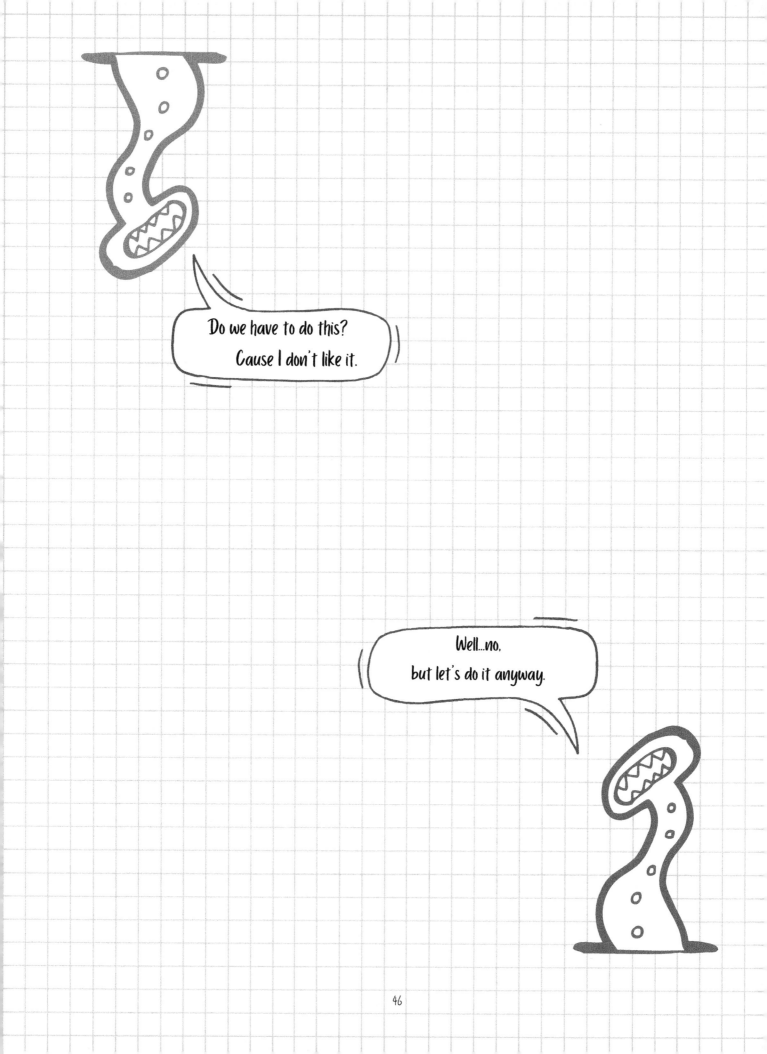

Here's a little hint: You are not the emotion.
You are the feeler of the feeling.
Example: You are not sad, you FEEL sad.
Start changing your language around emotions and see if you don't feel more in control of your feelings, and less overwhelmed by them.

If this feels overwhelming please take a break. Color something, take a walk, deep breathe, do a word search. This may seem simple, but emotions can brain ninjas.

Emotion List

In case your emotional vocabulary is a bit stunted (mine definitely was for a while), here are some feeling words to help you on your journey. Expanding your emotional vocabulary will be a far more valuable skill than you think.

Sad
Depressed
Dejected
Crushed
Upset
Sorrowful
Disappointed
Discouraged

Happy
Amused
Delighted
Glad
Content
Joyful
Loved
Pleased

Angry
Rage
Frustrated
Irritated
Jealous
Annoyed

Hurt
Betrayed
Wounded
Dismissed
Tender
Abused
Criticized
Rejected
Judged

Afraid
Stressed
Worthless
Guilty
Ashamed
Forced
Pressured
Attacked
Overwhelmed

Calm
Peaceful
Curious
Strong
Capable
Grounded
Healthy
Inspired
Creative
Focused

Tired
Bored
Drained
Numb
Sick
Uninterested
Exhausted
Weary
Fatigued

Insecure
Weak
Hopeless
Anxious
Worried
Embarrassed
Doubtful

I believe in you.

Emotion: _____

Date: _____

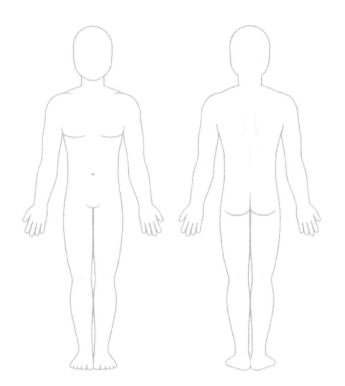

If this feeling had a color it would be:
_____
Descriptive words for this feeling:
_____
_____
_____

If this feeling was a song it would be:
_____
I tend to feel this when:
_____

How I feel about this feeling:
_____
_____
_____

Date: _____

Emotion: _____

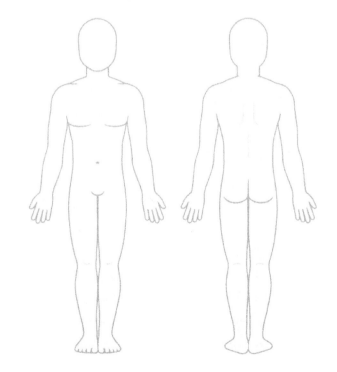

If this feeling had a color it would be:
_____
Descriptive words for this feeling:
_____
_____
_____

If this feeling was a song it would be:
_____
I tend to feel this when:
_____

How I feel about this feeling:
_____
_____
_____

Emotion: _____

Date: _____

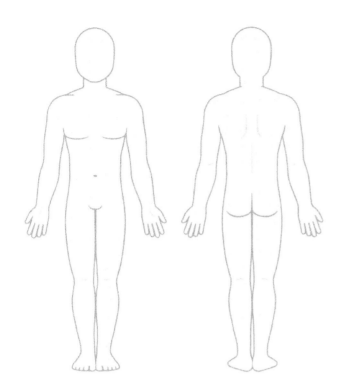

If this feeling had a color it would be:
_____

Descriptive words for this feeling:
_____
_____
_____

If this feeling was a song it would be:
_____

I tend to feel this when:
_____

How I feel about this feeling:
_____
_____
_____

Date: _____

Emotion: _____

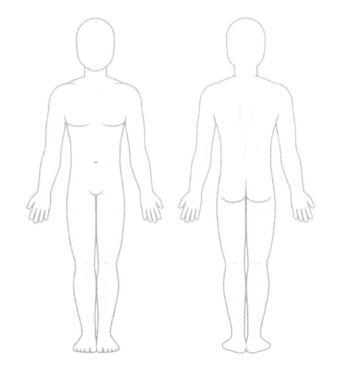

If this feeling had a color it would be:
_____

Descriptive words for this feeling:
_____
_____
_____

If this feeling was a song it would be:
_____

I tend to feel this when:
_____

How I feel about this feeling:
_____
_____
_____

Emotion: _____ Date: _____

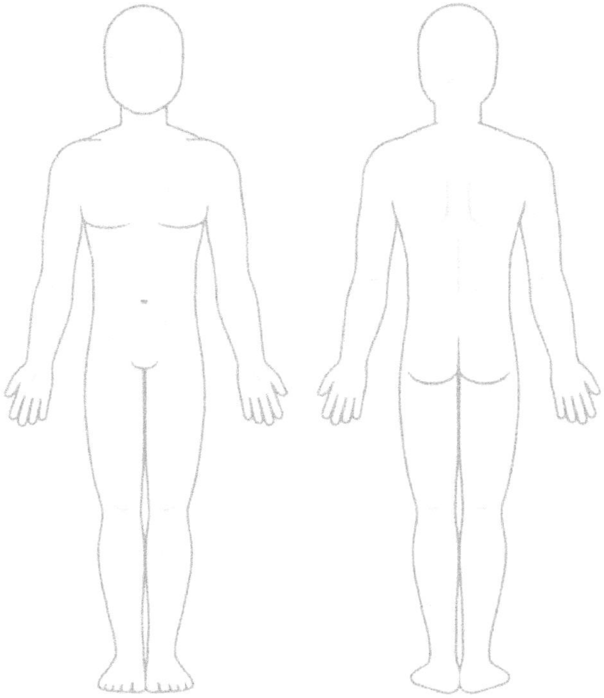

If this feeling had a color it would be:
_____

Descriptive words for this feeling:
_____
_____
_____

If this feeling was a song it would be:
_____

I tend to feel this when:
_____

How I feel about this feeling:
_____
_____
_____

Date: _____

If this feeling had a color it would be:
_____

Descriptive words for this feeling:
_____
_____
_____

If this feeling was a song it would be:
_____

I tend to feel this when:
_____

How I feel about this feeling:
_____
_____
_____

Emotion: _____

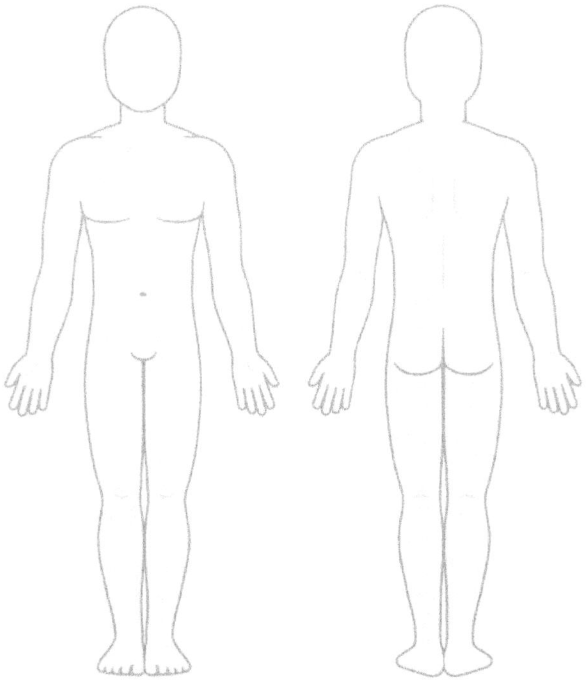

Emotion: _____ Date: _____

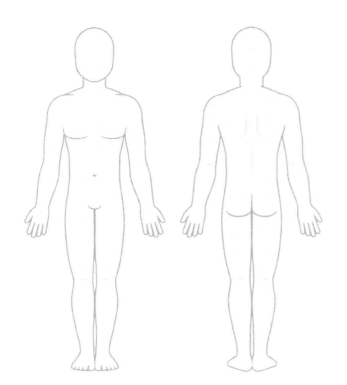

If this feeling had a color it would be:
_____

Descriptive words for this feeling:
_____
_____
_____

If this feeling was a song it would be:
_____

I tend to feel this when:
_____
_____

How I feel about this feeling:
_____
_____
_____

Date: _____

If this feeling had a color it would be:
_____

Descriptive words for this feeling:
_____
_____
_____

If this feeling was a song it would be:
_____

I tend to feel this when:
_____
_____

How I feel about this feeling:
_____
_____
_____

Emotion: _____

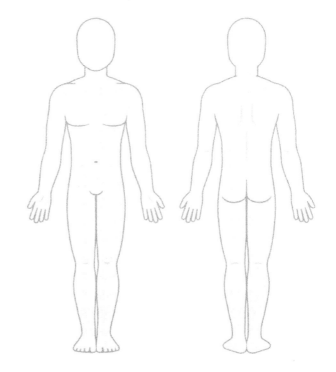

I am enough...
Just as I am...
Right now...

let's give this word-search a try

Emotions

```
U B D F L X F X J A N K S K Q V D B L U O Q U Q N
X Y N E M T F C O W F X W F Y E S F F V P Q M K O
F U H E H P W O Y F A Q C M N K L A B Y V O J T Z
X K P I J S C S F A V X S I I O V K T C G D N B B
G R L X T U I T U B R Q A L T H O E B H B R E B R
C E O F B M A R L V R R B L N S O U R T O E F P N
A V G M B O S E E Z D D V F R O I X O F Y O K X H
R A B M V C X S E H F P N E W I V M B V Y J C Q J
L N B N W C S K F C C I Y U N V H I V D E W F G
E W R K P W P E W W P D Z S F C D S O T D V M R G
F F B E R W Q D B K C E S W A I H G M I P G C Y X
I U A W B H Q E B X M T E G Z B R I C H C O O M N
K N M K M N E N L C A X K U P E G V H E C Y C K
X X N E L D O E G E K N K F N D V D U L K D L L C
X S R F Z R U I G E J L J E D I D O I E H I W S
O U A O K C Z A Y A S V L Y E S T G A E L G X V R
I Z S D E K M G X Z L U M M C D A G N S P T S Z U
K J J G Y N F V O A S J L O F X E T M N H P Y G S
J Q M C P R T L S S L E U C M N R B O H F A D J S
J R J N E A E Q U J H R J M L A C U G Q Q J M W I
V O W P I D C X E W A U K X N A N G R Y U O Q E G
K F S M A H L J R G P T L A K D Q V X G U P L G D
H N K E R B N E E T D E S U C O F F A L T C X B S
Y A W O T N V D X I Y E Z F G F K Z B O Q A O J O
U R U B G O D I K X U W S G A R W G H T S B G G L
```

ANGRY
JOYFUL
GUILTY
ASHAMED
CREATIVE
FOCUSED
OPTIMISTIC
CALM
STRESSED
WEAK
CHERISHED
DRAINED
DISCOURAGED
REJUVENATED
SAD
NEEDY
OVERWHELMED

Emotions are morally neutral
Not good or bad
Just information

Unpacking Stress

We all have different experiences with stress. There are massive, sudden events that turn our world inside-out, little repetitive daily stresses that bog us down, and slow-burn experiences that just seem to add more and more and more to our already full plates. The unfortunate problem with stress is that we don't get to decide whether or not we will have it in our lives. It is here, it must be dealt with, and it cannot be ignored. So, let's talk about it for a moment or two.

As a nurse, I can tell you that there are a whole bunch of hormones and neurotransmitters that go pinging through our bodies when we experience stress. This stress doesn't even have to be "bad" stress - good things can cause stress in our lives as well. For example: this book is a dream becoming reality in my life, but it is also stressful. Making sure that editing is complete, that the content is relatable, and worrying if you, my readers, will enjoy investing in your own development and growth in a meaningful way using the tools I've put in here. It's important and it matters to me, so I have some stress in regards to the book in your hands at this moment.

Stress can interfere with our thinking, our ability to carry out daily tasks, and totally interfere in our ability to get sleep. It has a wide and wild grip on our entire being. Many of us who grew up in chaotic households learned to minimize our perception of stress so that we could function. Unfortunately, this way of living became so normalized for us that we often have difficulty seeing how much stress we are actually living with. And because it is normalized, our happy little brains think it is how we *should* be doing life, so we tend to add stress to our lives when things are settling down, or we self-sabotage to increase the levels of stress we are working under. This cycle can become such a regular part of our lives that we don't even recognize it. It is time to break that cycle. The first step we gotta take is identifying our stress. Realistically. Like, an honest look at how much stress is really there. Buckle up friends - let's do this!

We can be stressed about good things too?
That doesn't seem fair...

Stress

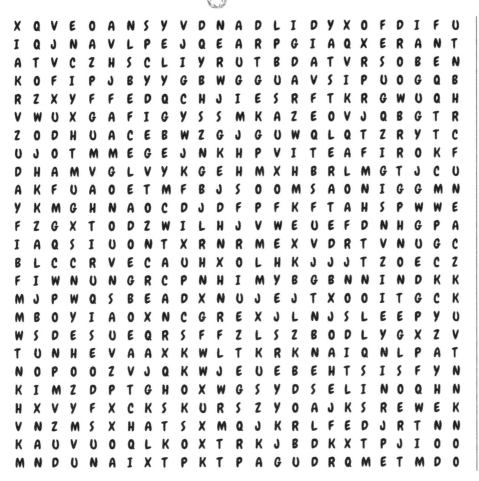

- TIRED
- DONE
- IRRITABLE
- ANGRY
- USED
- ANXIOUS
- TOLERATED
- SLEEPY
- TENSION
- DEADLINE
- EVENTS
- BAGGAGE
- TUNNEL
- FEELINGS
- NATURE
- SELFCARE

Don't let stress make you gnome, I mean, numb.

A little stress can help us get stuff done, but too much is not helpful. Maybe we can figure out how to balance that!

I have a theory that I call the Shit-stick theory of stress. It goes like this: every human has an internal shit stick. Most people have a stick that is about the size of a ruler - you know - 12 inches. At inch two or three, they realize that things are a bit stressful; at six or seven inches they start feeling overwhelmed and less able to get things done; and the danger zone is ten inches or above - this is when they might experience a bit of a mental breakdown because they are so overwhelmed they can't function. When chronic stress from chaos, abuse, or neglect were part of our "normal" day-to-day life growing up we still had to find a way to function, but if we tapped out at inch ten or eleven we would have been breaking down every single day. And as kiddos we didn't really have the option of simplifying our lives to reduce stress, so we did the only thing that we could - we made a bigger shit stick for ourselves.

This over-sized shit stick means that we can get a lot of stuff done before we have to wave the white flag in surrender. However, it also means that we tend to minimize what we are going through and the emotional impact it has on us. In order to decrease the size of our stick we have to get better at recognizing what we are going through, giving ourselves grace to feel our emotions about it, and being realistic about the potential need for assistance from our support people. These are all very difficult tasks, but worth doing.

The following exercise is a little more complex than some of the other ones in this book (two pages rather than just one). We are going to identify how much stress we are actually under. This is a great worksheet to complete when you hear yourself say the following words: "I don't know why I feel so anxious/stressed/down/overwhelmed. I don't know what is wrong with me lately."

As G.I. Joe used to say - "Knowing is half the battle!" I would also like to note here that if you struggle with issues such as anxiety, depression, or other mental health diagnosis, this can be a helpful way to to measure where you are emotionally/mentally in the present. We can use this language around work issues, home issues, relationship issues, etc. You can use the shit-stick analogy as a general life tool, or you can get specific with particular areas of your life. Find what works for you and see how much forward progress you can make just by learning how to identify the amount stress that is floating around in your life.

You are SO brave, and I am hella proud of you.

Unpacking Stress Part 1

Date: _____

First: identify an issue/event/relationship that is taking up space in your head and write it inside the "bag".
Second: pick the appropriate number for each of the accompanying statements.
Third: count those numbers for each item and write in the total for that stressor.

On a scale of 0-5, where 0 is "not so much" and 5 is "Make it Staaaahp"

This is on my mind like annoying background music that won't stop. _____
This feels urgent and unrelenting. _____
This is bringing up old "stuff" from the past for me. _____
This has multiple layers and/or long-term consequences. _____

This is on my mind like annoying background music that won't stop. _____
This feels urgent and unrelenting. _____
This is bringing up old "stuff" from the past for me. _____
This has multiple layers and/or long-term consequences. _____

This is on my mind like annoying background music that won't stop. _____
This feels urgent and unrelenting. _____
This is bringing up old "stuff" from the past for me. _____
This has multiple layers and/or long-term consequences. _____

Bag 1 total: _____   Bag 2 total: _____   Bag 3 total: _____

Let's take these numbers to the next page!

Date: _____

Unpacking Stress Part 2

Fourth: Label the ruler with your zones (these zone sizes will be unique to you).

Green zone: you are doing just fine and getting things done; you recognize some stress but it is not at the forefront of your mind.

Yellow zone: your stress is having an active effect on your daily functioning; you have trouble focusing, tasks seem too big, sounds are too loud, low-level agitation is constant.

Red zone: you are using all of your mental energy to make it through each moment; focusing is out of the question, and you feel panicked and overwhelmed.

Zones: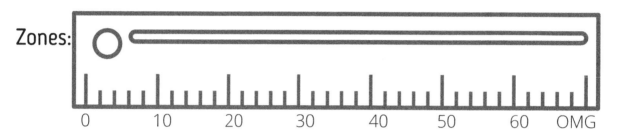

Fifth: Take those totals from Part 1 and color in your ruler...

MOST IMPORTANT STEP:

Oh my beautiful human! On top of all the daily tasks that must be completed, you are also dealing with THESE! That is so much. You are so amazing and deserve to have a solid cry, or a good scream into the void (or a pillow). We are going to validate your experience right now - say it out loud with me...

I am going through so much right now. I deserve to feel overwhelmed and upset. I deserve extra care and understanding - especially from myself. I am amazing and I deserve good things.

GOOD THING WE ARE TALKING ABOUT SELF-CARE NEXT. I THINK WE ALL NEED IT.

Unpacking Stress Part 1

Date: _____

First: identify an issue/event/relationship that is taking up space in your head and write it inside the "bag",
Second: pick the appropriate number for each of the accompanying statements.
Third: count those numbers for each item and write in the total for that stressor.

On a scale of 0-5, where 0 is "not so much" and 5 is "Make it Staaaahp"

This is on my mind like annoying background music that won't stop. _____
This feels urgent and unrelenting. _____
This is bringing up old "stuff" from the past for me. _____
This has multiple layers and/or long-term consequences. _____

This is on my mind like annoying background music that won't stop. _____
This feels urgent and unrelenting. _____
This is bringing up old "stuff" from the past for me. _____
This has multiple layers and/or long-term consequences. _____

This is on my mind like annoying background music that won't stop. _____
This feels urgent and unrelenting. _____
This is bringing up old "stuff" from the past for me. _____
This has multiple layers and/or long-term consequences. _____

Bag 1 total: _____   Bag 2 total: _____   Bag 3 total: _____

Let's take these numbers to the next page!

Date: _____

Unpacking Stress Part 2

Fourth: Label the ruler with your zones (these zone sizes will be unique to you).
  Green zone: you are doing just fine and getting things done; you recognize some stress but it is not at the forefront of your mind.
  Yellow zone: your stress is having an active effect on your daily functioning; you have trouble focusing, tasks seem too big, sounds are too loud, low-level agitation is constant.
  Red zone: you are using all of your mental energy to make it through each moment; focusing is out of the question, and you feel panicked and overwhelmed.

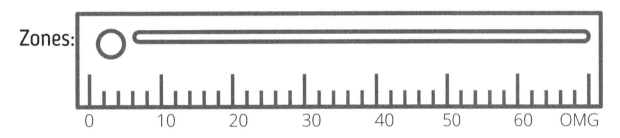

Zones:

Fifth: Take those totals from Part 1 and color in your ruler…

Most Important Step:

Oh my beautiful human! On top of all the daily tasks that must be completed, you are also dealing with THESE! That is so much. You are so amazing and deserve to have a good cry, or a good scream into the void (or a pillow). I want to validate your experience right now - say it out loud with me…

I am going through so much right now. I deserve to feel overwhelmed and upset. I deserve extra care and understanding - especially from myself. I am amazing and I deserve good things.

TIME FOR A BRAIN BREAK:
THREE DEEP BREATHS
WALK OUTSIDE FOR 10 MIN
PLAY WITH A PET
HAVE A CUP OF TEA/COFFEE

Self-Care

Let's talk about how to reduce stress, and increase our capacity in an area that is highly important and often misunderstood. Self-care is not always "treat yo' self" although it can be; it is not always bubble baths and a glass of your favorite beverage, although it can be; it is not just drinking your water, although that is part of it (I'm guessing you might be picking up on a pattern at this point). There are some self-care tasks that are priorities for all humans and should be attended to on a daily basis, others that you can pull out of your hat for those especially rough days, and some that you do more regularly for maintenance. Self-care is going to look different for everyone, but we can identify some umbrella categories and then drill down into specifics. The following activity is going to help you identify some self-care tasks that work for YOU. If you're anything like me, it might be tough to figure out what self-care looks like and what you *want* it to look like. I have been a chronic care-giver/co-dependent/whatever-label-you-wanna-use for the majority of my life, so it was hysterically difficult to figure out how to do this whole self-care thing. It can feel intimidating and remarkably selfish to create a list of things that you are going to do for YOURSELF, but as Glennon Doyle says: "We can do hard things."

Also of note: you may not be able to do self-care tasks in the most ideal way each and every time. There might be financial constraints, or emotional fatigue that limits what you are able to complete, or just plain time issues, but...please remember that self-care is a *practice*, so you may not be good at it to begin with and it might be easier some days than others - and that's okay. Here are some basic life "modes" and what self-care can look like when we are in those places.

Survival Mode: These are the absolute basics and include things like: drinking 32oz of water, eating at least one meal daily, getting 5 hours of sleep, brushing your teeth, or doing a quick washcloth bath. This might look like changing into clean pajamas, or brushing your hair. Give yourself credit for the immense strength it takes to move through survival.
Struggle Mode: This level includes things like: attending therapy, calling a friend, reaching out to your support group, going to the doctors office. Setting a goal to eat two meals a day, changing your sheets and doing some laundry. Taking a shower or bath falls under this category. We are doing more than surviving here - but not a whole lot more. This stage is still a lot of hard work to navigate, so be graceful with yourself (stop beating yourself up for being where you are).
Maintenance Mode: Here is where we start to see some of the fun self-care start. You might want to take yourself out to coffee, or enjoy some hot tea while listening to music on the back porch. This might look like starting a new journal, or meeting with some friends. Maintenance mode is when our basic human needs are mostly being met and we can add some "fill-the-cup" activities to our day-to-day schedule without feeling overwhelmed. Some of these tasks may not be super fun but they also tend to be ones that "tomorrow-me" will appreciate like: getting laundry folded and put away, tidying up my room, cleaning the bathroom or making sure the kitchen is clean enough to use for the next meal.
Recovery Mode: Any self-care tasks in this mode are my fallback list for when I need a little extra to get me through the day and prevent me from falling into struggle mode or survival mode. This tends to be on post-therapy days, or high stress days. It can be when an anniversary of one of my trauma experiences comes around and I just need...extra. For me this list includes buying a new book to read, or some new yarn to play with. It can look like planning a day away from home/children/job and enjoying stress-free time in nature or in the library; could be watching my favorite show for a few hours and zoning out. Any activity that gives me that little extra boost that I need.

I added dancing to Every. Single. Category. It doesn't have to be pretty or coordinated, but make moving your body a priority every day. It helps our nervous system, our joints, our mental health, and ALL THE THINGS. You can do one 3 min song. I believe in you.

The following exercise can be utilized in conjunction with your shit-stick exercise, or all by itself. Let's figure out what your self-care cup looks like.

What are some of your favorite songs?

Survive

Drink 32oz of water
Get a minimum of ___ hours of sleep
Eat something
Change into clean clothes
Brush hair and brush teeth

 Dance through 1 song

Struggle

 Dance through 1 song

Maintain

Dance 10-20 minutes

Recover

Dance 10-20 minutes

Don't beat yourself up if self-care is really tricky at first, especially if you're in survival mode. GENTLE, my little cupcake!

Self Care

```
R E V O C E R F J E L G G U R T S I H F Z P N V Q
D D M R Y M P Y D V U B M Y N B S S W C E K C B J
G A H P Y S L Y D E S P U C D Q Q Z B E R R V P Q
G M F E Q M S L O M W U G B A A U D L T Y P P K S
P C X U N J Q E A O Q X K R O R N S K B R F F U H
I C D P D V B S M X B A K U T U O E N O Z A M X Q
G V X W N H S D N B G M Y I O F H M R S S L P K S
M K B H N A F Q C X S Q Q O H A E W O D A P A U Z
Y E V T G B E K C P H U H V B F V E S U V I R T T
S W W E K K W I P A C Y Y S P Q G B V Q P V X P W
C B F V D M K Y N L Y P T E V R E J N K I W I V Q
F U C W K U W H W A F N V D U Z A U I V N M Z R R
V Y J N I M Q L B C E H A P D D K C A S S L O V R
N R V M D I K A U M H C R J G E S L T W W T V H X
R C M X X P Z U T N Z A T H Y U H E N I U Q E C Y
B Z U Z J W K N V V M T M H J E W M I P C X I I D
T Q Q D W F I D T B V N C G B V C Z A V W E R N A
C P J F O O D R R M W N L C H X N T M F O R E S N
S U V K P F S Y F M K K I C E O V L E Y E M A T C
Y Y R P C N X D S A H B P R L Q K N I F M A D J E
Q X A I D D I A M H U C F R E T A W R O H E I L V
G H F C B W M H K R K A B T O A H E V S X Q N Q M
G D A M H S P M B S T P A T D U S T U N C U G P X
G P W A Y Q P X U C Q J Q H M H Q R J Q A W V K D
H T N D I J P D U E X X Y G U U B V A M Q G X V Y
```

DANCE
WATER
FOOD
SURVIVAL
STRUGGLE
MAINTAIN
RECOVER
LAUNDRY
APPOINTMENTS
SLEEP
CUPS
MESSY
PRACTICE
BRUSH
MASSAGE
READING
MOVIES
ZONEOUT
REFRESH

Did you know that we are comforted by re-watching shows or movies we've seen before? We know what's coming next, so it can help calm our anxiety. What are your favorite shows or movies to re-watch?

Self-care Tracker

(HELPFUL FOR WHEN YOU ARE FIGURING THIS STUFF OUT)

Today (_____/_____/_____),
I am in _____ mode.
I will complete the following self-care tasks today because I deserve good things:

_____
_____
_____

My mantra today is:
Wherever I am mentally today is okay.
It is a morally neutral state (it is not good or bad, it simply is).
I will do what I can and know that it is enough. I am enough.

Today (_____/_____/_____),
I am in _____ mode.
I will complete the following self-care tasks today because I deserve good things:

_____
_____
_____

My mantra today is:

_____
_____
_____

Self-care Tracker

(HELPFUL FOR WHEN YOU ARE FIGURING THIS STUFF OUT)

Today (_____/_____/_____),
I am in _____ mode.
I will complete the following self-care tasks today because I deserve good things:
_____
_____
_____

My mantra today is:
_____
_____
_____

Today (_____/_____/_____),
I am in _____ mode.
I will complete the following self-care tasks today because I deserve good things:
_____
_____
_____

My mantra today is:
_____
_____
_____

If I am having trouble figuring out how to take care of myself, I can look at the things I do for other people when I know they are struggling and then do those things for myself!

Self-care Tracker
(HELPFUL FOR WHEN YOU ARE FIGURING THIS STUFF OUT)

Today (___/___/___),
I am in _____ mode.
I will complete the following self-care tasks today because I deserve good things:
_____
_____
_____

My mantra today is:
_____
_____
_____

What do you think? Are you noticing any changes? Hard things? Good things?

Thank you for joining me on a little mental health adventure. This "activity book for adults" was a ton of fun to put together and I already have four or five more just waiting to transition from my head onto paper. Stay tuned for Moms on the Edge coming soon.

Remember: you are an amazing human, who deserves love and belonging, and you are wonderful just the way you are. Healing is a dance, not a light switch; and it's almost always more fun when we know we aren't doing it alone.

Recommended Reading List

- Anything by Brene' Brown including any of her books, her Netflix special, her two podcasts, etc. She specializes in the study of shame, and her books completely transformed my life by teaching me how to heal my sense of self, find my resiliency, and how to be brave.
- Glennon Doyle's books "Untamed", and "Love Warrior". These explore what it means to be human, and particularly how we define love and life. She also started a podcast, and it is excellent so go check it out.
- Abby Wombach's "Wolf Pack" ~ taught me to change my perspective around what it means to be part of a community.
- Jenny Lawson's "Broken", "Let's Pretend This Never Happened", and "Furiously Happy". Jenny feels like a kindred spirit who struggles just like we do. Her books are hilarious, touching, and delightfully weird.
- Felicia Day's "You're Never Weird on the Internet (Almost)" was a super relatable book and felt very validating.

Made in the USA
Las Vegas, NV
08 July 2021